TIBOR RUDAS PRESENTS

CARRERAS ~ DOMINGO ~ PAVAROTTI

TENORS
3

WITH MEHTA ~ IN CONCERT 1994

CollinsPublishersSanFrancisco

A Division of HarperCollinsPublishers

TIBOR RUDAS WELCOME 11

≈

INTRODUCTION 12

≈

THE PERFORMERS 15

≈

THE ORCHESTRA 32

≈

THE CHORUS 33

≈

THE TRANSFORMATION 35

≈

THE PERFORMANCE 61

≈

THE CONCERT PROGRAM 85

≈

TRIBUTE 117

≈

CREDITS 122

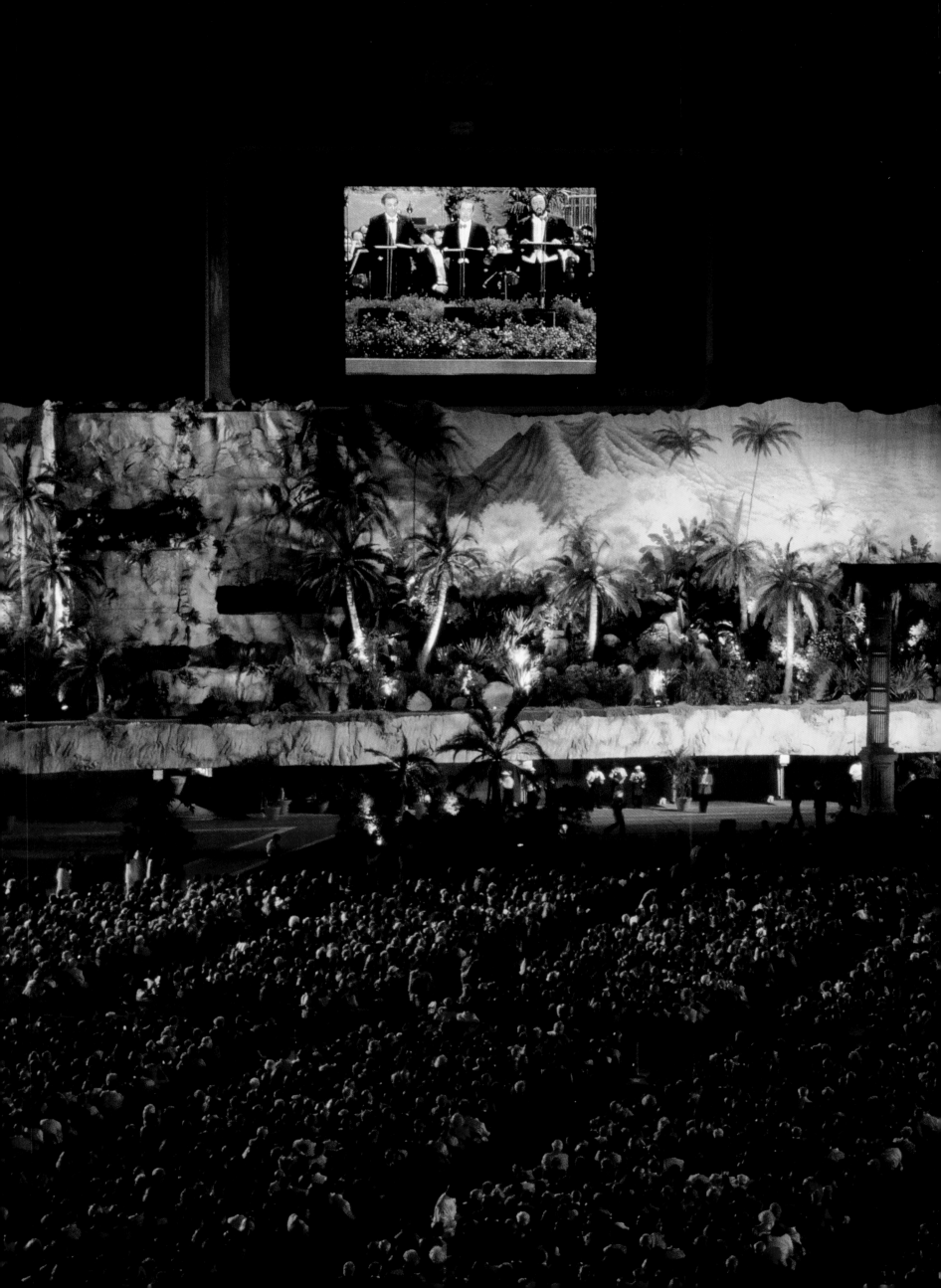

This beautiful volume is a memento of an exceptional event—the historic reunion of THE THREE TENORS IN CONCERT 1994.

There isn't a producer in the world who wouldn't have cherished the opportunity to present this extraordinary gathering of talent. Nor is there a country on the planet that wouldn't have wanted to be the host of such an important event. I am very proud to have been given that great honor, and prouder still that the concert happened in Los Angeles, the world's entertainment capital.

Perhaps you were there among the fifty-six thousand ecstatic participants at the stadium. Or maybe you were a member of the worldwide audience, watching or listening along with well over a billion more who were able to enjoy the concert as it was transmitted in television and radio broadcasts. From whatever our individual vantage, we can all reflect on that brilliant evening knowing that we were privileged participants in one of the landmark events marking the close of the twentieth century.

The excitement surrounding the concert had been building for months, and more than fifty thousand tickets were sold long in advance of the event — most of them to an audience that had never been inside an opera house, but which loved these artists through their recordings and television appearances. If only a handful of this audience has been inspired to visit an opera house for the first time because of this performance, then these maestros have furthered my dream of extending opera to the general public.

I cannot give enough thanks to the hundreds of artists and technical experts, as well as to the hundreds of other co-workers - and most importantly, to the staff of the Rudas Organization, whose two years of preparation made this concert possible.

I would like to extend my deepest gratitude to Mr. Ahmet Ertegun and Mr. Alan Rothenberg of World Cup USA 1994, for selecting this performance as the "Final Concert" of the world's greatest sporting event. And my gratitude also extends to Mr. Peter O'Malley, President of the Los Angeles Dodgers, for having had the foresight to know that their beautiful stadium would be naturally suited for the transformation into a spectacular amphitheater. They and their magnificent staffs made the dream a reality.

It gives me great pleasure to share with you this remembrance of an extraordinary performance by artists who are not just for our time, but forever.

Enjoy the memories!

Tibor Rudas

On July 16, 1994, the moon shone down on Los Angeles to reveal an astounding sight: Dodger Stadium was transformed from ballpark to amphitheater, where four gifted musicians gathered to enthrall an audience. The conjunction of these stellar performers in concert together created a kind of spontaneous combustion, a brilliant explosion radiating an excitement rarely seen in the world of classical music. And they came together not just as colleagues, but as friends — and friendly competitors.

Music was not the only tie to bind them. They are all passionate fans of the single most popular sport in the world — soccer. As José Carreras put it, "it's not just a sport but a social phenomenon!" It was the World Cup

Finals in 1990 that drew them together for the first time in Rome. They then waited for four years to repeat their collaboration, rejecting almost daily offers to perform together. For Plácido Domingo, "The event could have taken place anywhere, but the best place was Dodger Stadium..." to sing in celebration of their lifelong love affair with soccer.

The singers rooted for the teams of their home countries - Spain for Domingo and Carreras and Italy for Pavarotti. "We did it for the Cup," says Luciano Pavarotti, emphasizing their collective affection for the game. When asked which of

the teams he supported, the ever diplomatic Bombay-born Zubin Mehta responded, "In my country, we play cricket! My main concern was that if Spain and Italy were playing against each other in the final match the day after the concert, my conducting job would have been that much harder!"

To make this concert possible, the four principal artists were surrounded and supported by a huge team of nearly 1000 musicians, performers, artisans, craftsmen, technicians, engineers, and other staff. An estimated 1.3 billion television viewers in more than 100 countries made the concert the most watched worldwide music event of all time. To make the videocassette and laserdisc versions of the concert even more unique and dynamic, video recordings were made from fourteen isolated cameras and edited together to capture the vast scope of the event. To satisfy public demand, both the audio and video recording formats were released in record time — within one month — by Atlantic Records in the United States and Teldec Classics internationally. A behind-the-scenes documentary was also produced in order to share the varied activities of two years of planning.

With the global audience in mind, the four principal artists conceived the concert program with care. The arias and songs they performed are among the most beautiful ever composed and the favorites of fans everywhere. They are the songs that inspire us, brighten our spirits, and move our hearts.

~ THE PERFORMERS ~

JOSÉ CARRERAS:

"We are four colleagues, and we have lots of respect and admiration for each other. But first of all, we are four very, very good friends, and we know very well the incredible joy each of us feels singing with the others on stage. We all believe in this concert, and I think that this is the main reason why we decided to sing together again."

J OSÉ CARRERAS holds a singular place among today's most celebrated tenors. Acclaimed for the rich, natural lyricism of his voice and an arresting intensity of delivery, Mr. Carreras has brought a distinctive sensibility to the opera stage.

He was born on December 5, 1947, in the Spanish region of Catalonia, known for its proud and individualistic people. An irrepressible performer as a boy, his natural vocal gifts were apparent from an early age as he sang along with the recordings of Mario Lanza and Giuseppe di Stefano. At age eleven, on the stage of the famed Gran Teatro del Liceo in Barcelona under the baton of José Iturbi, he made his operatic debut as the narrator in de Falla's *Master Peter's Puppet Show*.

Although certain his career would be on the opera stage, he pursued a more practical curriculum at the University of Barcelona, studying chemistry and intending to join in the family cosmetics concern. Still, the voice lessons continued, and his fate was sealed in 1971 when he won the International Verdi Singing Competition in Parma, Italy. The prize included an engagement as Rodolfo in *La*

Bohème; a performance that prompted rapturous ovations from the demanding Teatro Regio audience.

He made his international debut in a concert performance of Donizetti's *Maria Stuarda* at Festival Hall, London, in 1971. Successes in important roles at opera houses around the world soon broadened his reputation. He sang his first Pinkerton in *Madama Butterfly* with the New York City Opera in 1972; his Metropolitan Opera debut as Cavaradossi in *Tosca* came in 1974, the same year he triumphed at London's Covent Garden, Vienna's Staatsoper, and Milan's La Scala in *Un Ballo in Maschera*. By 1975, he had conquered all of the world's leading stages.

Herbert von Karajan invited Mr. Carreras to sing in Verdi's *Requiem* during the 1976 Salzburg Easter Festival. Performances and recordings of various works followed, during which the maestro and the tenor cultivated an intense artistic collaboration and close friendship that was to last the next twelve years.

CARR

Recent triumphs include *Fedora* at La Scala and Verdi's *Stiffelio* at Covent Garden, a universally acclaimed performance for which he was awarded the 1992/93 Sir Laurence Olivier Award. He also served as Musical Director for the opening and closing ceremonies of the 1992 Summer Olympic Games in his beloved native Barcelona.

Over the course of his career, Mr. Carreras has made a prodigious number of recordings, including more than 50 complete operas and 40 classical and popular recitals. He has forayed into lighter reper-toire, encompassing Spanish and Italian songs, works by Andrew

Lloyd Webber, Rodgers and Hammerstein's *South Pacific*, the multi-ple-award-winning recording *West Side Story*, conducted by its composer Leonard Bernstein, and a tribute to his early vocal inspiration, Mario Lanza. Several of these recordings have achieved gold and platinum status. Many video recordings of his performances in leading roles are also available. His video por-trait, *A Life Story*, won the International Emmy Award. He has also made a motion picture, *Romanza Final*, in which he portrays the life of tenor Julian Gayarre.

Public awareness of his struggle against a near fatal encounter with leukemia in 1987 inspired millions with his courage.

In 1988, The José Carreras International Leukemia Foundation was established in Barcelona. With the collaboration of a highly qualified worldwide team, including Professor E. D. Thomas, the winner of the 1990 Nobel Prize for Medicine, Mr. Carreras success-fully governs his organization as its president. His autobiography, *José Carreras, Singing From the Soul*, tells the extraordinary story of his life and career, his illness, and his devotion to his family and children.

José Carreras is a hero for our time, a sensitive artist and courageous humanitarian who has enriched the world with his considerable gifts.

PLÁCIDO DOMINGO:

❝You can see that each one is breathing for the other one when he is singing, because we know how difficult it is, and I think the success of one reflects in the general success. We all want to really be in the most friendly situation at the time we are performing. But as dangerous as it is for us to be singing in front of millions of people, I'd rather be one of the Three Tenors with Maestro Mehta conducting than be one of the goalkeepers in the finals!**❞**

PLÁCIDO DOMINGO stands at the pinnacle of a career that spans virtually every role in the tenor repertoire and is honored and celebrated by millions of admiring fans around the world. He is a peerless singing actor whose burnished voice is instantly recognizable and renowned for its power, depth, and subtlety.

He was born in Madrid on January 21, 1941. His parents, popular zarzuela performers, formed their own company and moved the family to Mexico City when he was eight; his early musical education included experiences performing in their productions. As a student he enjoyed soccer, playing goalkeeper on his school team. Among his classmates, three became professional players, including World Cup player José Luis González.

Plácido Domingo began his career singing in his parents' zarzuelas, and he even had a part in the Mexican première of *My Fair Lady*. In 1959, after a successful audition with the Mexican National Opera, he began to master the operatic repertory and debuted in *La Traviata* in Monterrey in 1961. The Israel National Opera offered him a six-month engagement in 1962; there he thrived during the next two and a half years, singing 280 performances in 12 leading roles.

Successful performances in the United States in 1965 preceded his New York City Opera debut in *Madama Butterfly* on October 17. He made his debut at the Metropolitan Opera on September 28, 1968, in *Adriana Lecouvreur*. In the twenty-five years since, he has sung more performances at the Met than in any other opera house in the world and more opening nights at the Met than anyone since Caruso. In 1993, he and Luciano Pavarotti celebrated their 25th anniversaries there together with a glittering Opening Night Gala.

Plácido Domingo regularly performs in the world's leading opera houses, singing a truly amazing number of Italian and French roles. His ever-expanding foray into the repertoire has resulted in the recordings of a number of German roles: *Meistersinger, Lohengrin, Tannhäuser, the Flying Dutchman*, and the Emperor in *Die Frau ohne Schatten*. Onstage performances of German roles include *Lohengrin, Parsifal*, Siegmund in *Die Walküre*, and an upcoming performance as Tristan in 1996. He constantly challenges himself by learning new roles and

champions new works, performing in such varied compositions as *Don Rodrigo* by Alberto Ginastera, which inaugurated the New York State Theatre at Lincoln Center in 1966, and *Goya*, written for him by Gian Carlo Menotti, which had its world première in Washington, D.C., in 1986.

He is a prolific recording artist, so far releasing 87 complete performances of 59 different operas and numerous solo and duet discs, eight of which have received Grammy Awards. He is as much at home with the popular repertoire as with the classics. *Perhaps Love*, recorded with John Denver, sold several million copies worldwide, and other successful crossover albums followed. He has starred in three acclaimed opera films, Zeffirelli's *La Traviata* and *Otello* and Rossi's *Carmen*. He is often seen in televised performances, including his Emmy-winning appearances in *Plácido Domingo Celebrates Seville* and *The Metropolitan Opera Silver Anniversary Gala*. In July of 1992, he portrayed Cavaradossi in an Emmy-winning pro-

duction of *Tosca*, broadcast live from its three historic Roman locations.

Although "Plácido Domingo" might translate from Spanish into English as "peaceful Sunday," his life is anything but. He has simultaneously pursued a successful conducting career nearly as long as his operatic one, leading performances in major opera houses and concert halls since making his conducting debut with *La Traviata* at the New York City Opera during its 1973–74 season. He employs his considerable managerial skills as Artistic Consultant to the Los Angeles Music Center Opera and was Music Director for the 1992 Seville World's Fair.

Closer to the heart, his tireless philanthropic efforts on behalf of the 1985 Mexican earthquake victims have raised millions of dollars.

Whether thrilling an opera house audience with his voice, inspiring an orchestra from the podium, or employing his expertise to bring new productions to the stage, Plácido Domingo is a renaissance man in the truest sense of the word.

INGO

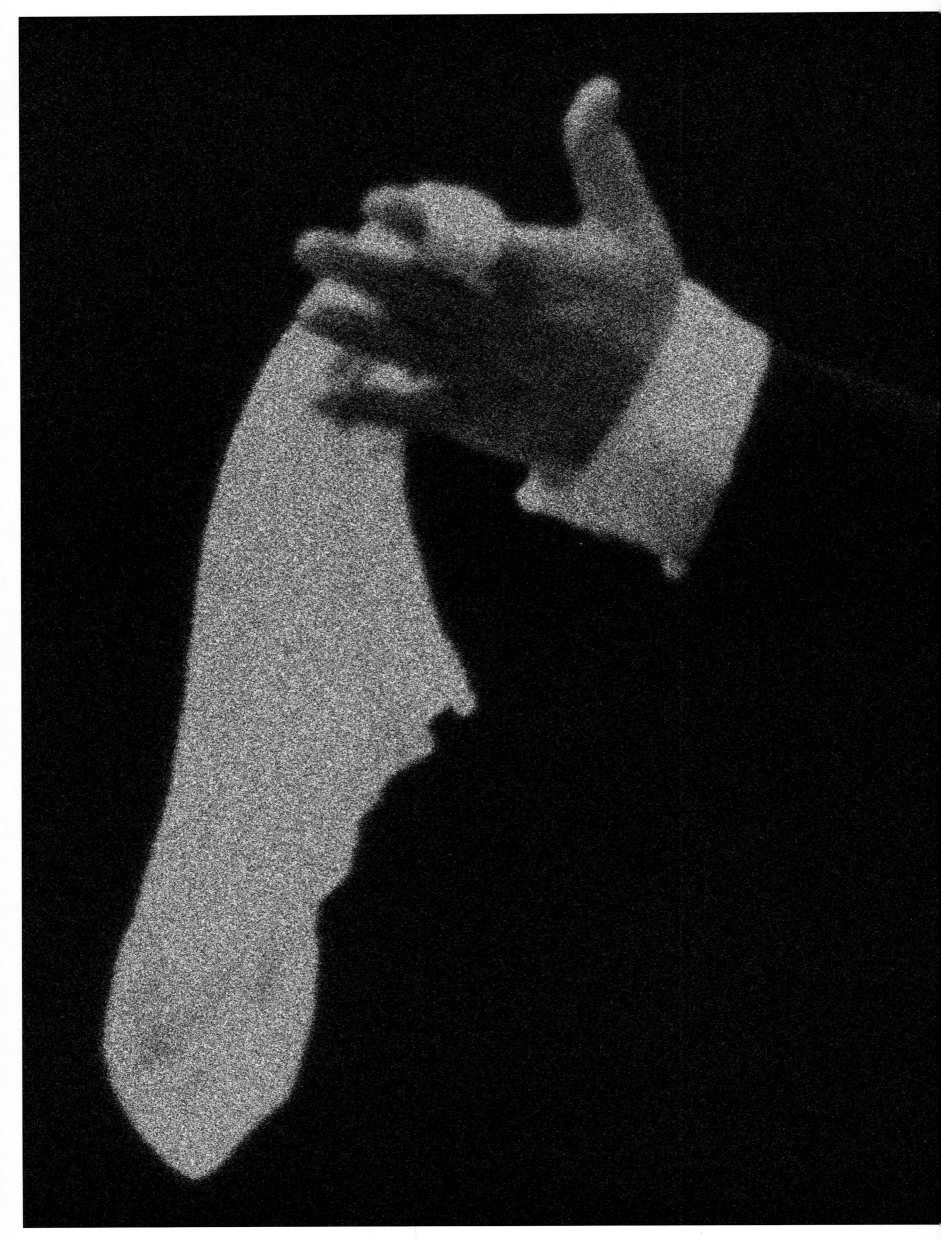

66 For one second before I sing, I am thinking about something else. I am thinking about my father, who is the most severe critic in the world. Am I going to please him or not? I'm serious! My father is a tenor, and he's very tough. Very, very tough. He's 81 now, and he is still singing quite beautifully. 99

LUCIANO PAVAROTTI makes an immense impact on the world of classical music, broadening its horizons and attracting countless fans. Thanks to his thrilling voice and unique personality, the name "Pavarotti" has become a household word, synonymous with the highest standards of performance.

He was born in Modena, Italy, on October 12, 1935, the first child and only son of a baker. As a boy, sports occupied much of his time. In fact, he earned his first local fame as a member of the town's soccer team, excelling at the game he has followed passion-

ately ever since. He first sang in the Modena chorus with his father, a fervent lover of opera and gifted amateur tenor. When the chorus won first prize in an international competition, the youngster was hooked.

His debut came on April 29, 1961, as Rodolfo in *La Bohème*, at the opera house in Reggio Emilia. That success led to engagements throughout Italy and the world, where he conquered audiences in Amsterdam, Vienna, Zurich, and London. His American debut came

in February, 1965, in a Miami production of *Lucia di Lammermoor* with Joan Sutherland, the beginning of what would become their historic partnership. Debuts in *La Bohème* at La Scala, San Francisco, and New York won the hearts of fans around the world.

But it wasn't until February 17, 1972, that the Pavarotti phenomenon was born, in a production of *La Fille du Régiment* at New York's Metropolitan Opera. Responding to Pavarotti's aria containing nine effortless high Cs, the audience erupted in a frenzied ovation, and the young tenor's reputation soared into the stratosphere.

Maestro Pavarotti appears on the greatest international opera and concert stages, collaborating with the world's most gifted conductors and singers, on television, in movies, and in arena concerts. His recordings, each and every one a best-seller, include collections of arias and recital programs, a live concert from Carnegie Hall, and anthologies of Neapolitan and other Italian songs.

His frequent television appearances in performance as well as

PAVA

in documentaries and on talk shows continue to add to his musical renown. His performance as Rodolfo thrilled America in the historic first *Live from the Met* telecast in March of 1977, which attracted one of the largest audiences ever for a televised opera. And from that same stage, he and Plácido Domingo together celebrated their 25th anniversaries with an Opening Night Gala performance in the fall of 1993.

He consistently draws record-breaking audiences to sold-out arena concerts in many countries and shares his music with huge audiences in the great public parks of the world. His televised concert in London's Hyde Park, in the presence of Charles and Diana, the Prince and Princess of Wales, was the first concert in the history of the park featuring classical music and drew a record attendance of some 150,000 people. In June 1993, more than 500,000 fans gathered to enjoy his performance on the Great Lawn of New York's Central Park, while millions more around the world watched on television. The following September, singing in the shadow of the Eiffel Tower in Paris, he thrilled the hearts of an estimated 300,000 music lovers.

Maestro Pavarotti is also dedicated to the development of the careers of young singers. In 1982 he initiated an ongoing international vocal competition culminating with prestigious final performances in Philadelphia. He also conducts standing-room-only master classes at conservatories around the world.

He still makes his home in Modena, taking time each summer for a retreat to his vacation home in Pesaro, a converted farmhouse overlooking the Adriatic. There he relaxes with his wife, Adua, and

their three daughters, other family members, and friends, preparing sumptuous meals with the region's excellent food and wine and riding his horses in the surrounding countryside.

Illuminated by his radiant personality and propelled by his zest for life Luciano Pavarotti's golden voice transcends the walls of the opera house to reach inside every human heart and mind.

ZUBIN MEHTA:

" I'm flying on a magic carpet with them. As an accompanist, as a man who makes music with them, I have such confidence. Sometimes when you work with a soloist, either instrumental or a singer, you feel you have to be careful in case something goes wrong. With them, it just doesn't happen, and it's a great satisfaction. They don't know what a fan I am. It's just pleasure from the beginning—from the planning stages. "

ZUBIN MEHTA has achieved a unique position among conductors in the world today. He was born in Bombay, India on April 29, 1936. His parents discouraged his early interest in becoming a classical musician, even though his father, Mehli Mehta, was a violinist and co-founder of the Bombay Symphony. Mr. Mehta was to study medicine; but by the age of eighteen, the die was cast when he had the chance to lead his father's orchestra in several performances. He soon abandoned his medical studies to pursue his musical destiny at the Academy of Music in Vienna.

Seven years later, at the remarkably young age of twenty-five,

he had conducted both the Vienna and Berlin Philharmonics, and, from 1961 to 1967, acted as Music Director of the Montreal Symphony. In 1962, the Los Angeles Philharmonic appointed him Music Director, a post he held for sixteen years; this concert is a happy reunion with that great orchestra. He accepted the appointment of Music Director with the New York Philharmonic in 1978, serving with them until 1991.

In 1961, a lifelong bond was begun when he first led the Israel Philharmonic Orchestra. He was appointed its Music Advisor in 1969, Music Director in 1977, and, in 1981, its Music Director for Life. Numerous concerts, recordings, and tours of all five continents have generated more than 1500 concerts with that orchestra.

During his thirteen year tenure with the New York Philharmonic, Maestro Mehta conducted more than 1000 concerts and held the post longer than any music director in the Orchestra's modern history. During his tenure, he conducted the Philharmonic on a number of major tours covering all five continents. The tour especially dear to his heart was to Asia in 1984, which culminated in his home town of Bombay. In June 1988 he led a ten-day visit to the Soviet Union that included an historic joint concert with the State Symphony Orchestra of the Soviet Ministry of Culture in Moscow's Gorky Park. In May 1991, the Maestro concluded his tenure with three performances celebrating the 100th anniversary of Carnegie

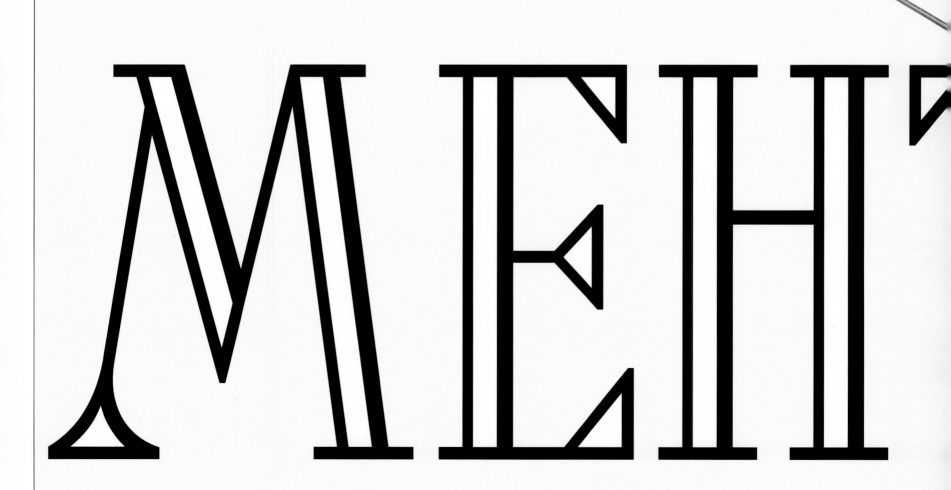

MEH

Hall, followed by a series of performances of Schoenberg's *Gurrelieder*. In the fall of 1992, he returned to conduct the world premier of Olivier Messiaen's last symphony, "*Èclairs sur l'Au Delá,*" and joined in the Philharmonic's 150th Anniversary Concert.

His love of opera has led to many productions, including Puccini's Tosca with Luciano Pavarotti at Covent Garden.His 1993 debut with the Lyric Opera of Chicago commenced a four-year commitment to conduct Wagner's "Ring" cycle. Since 1986, he has also acted as Music Advisor and Chief Conductor to the Maggio Musicale Fiorentino, a renowned summer festival in Florence. There, he recently completed a cycle of Mozart operas, produced under the direction of Jonathan Miller.

Maestro Mehta is also known to audiences through his frequent appearances on *Live from Lincoln Center* and other television broadcasts. In July 1992, he joined forces with Plácido Domingo and Catherine Malfitano in an unprecedented live telecast of *Tosca*, performed at the locations and at the exact times of day specified in the score. The broadcast was seen in 107 countries and won him his second Emmy.

During the past twenty years, Mr. Mehta has done extensive concert, opera and recording work with tenors Carreras, Domingo and Pavarotti, including: an upcoming première of Verdi's *Jerusalem* with Mr. Carreras at the Vienna State Opera, Puccini's *Girl of the Golden West* and *Tosca* and Verdi's *Il Trovatore* with Mr. Domingo, and a legendary recording of *Turandot* with Mr. Pavarotti.

Today, Mr. Mehta continues his busy schedule leading major orchestras and opera companies the world over, including the London, Vienna and Berlin Philharmonics, the Vienna Staatsoper, and of course, the Israel Philharmonic Orchestra.

For more than 75 years, the Los Angeles Philharmonic has brought pride to the citizens of Los Angeles with a diverse roster of musical performances that is enjoyed by more than one million concert-goers annually. The orchestra has developed steadily in artistic stature and prominence since its founding in 1919 and ranks among the world's leading international symphonic organizations. The brilliant Finnish conductor Esa-Pekka Salonen, now into his third season as Music Director, leads the Philharmonic toward the next century as it looks forward to the move into its new home in the Walt Disney Concert Hall. Nine other renowned conductors have led the orchestra since its founding, including the recent tenures of André Previn and Carlo Maria Giulini. The performance at Dodger Stadium reunited the orchestra with another of its celebrated music directors, Zubin Mehta, who served the longest, from 1962 until 1978.

The orchestra has a commitment to share a broad range of the musical repertoire in order to satisfy the diverse tastes of its audience. Giving some 300 concerts, recitals, and special programs each season, it regularly performs an impressive variety of music, from the masterworks of Mozart, Beethoven, and Tchaikovsky to premières by important living composers. Its musicians participate in a variety of chamber music and contemporary music concerts, community activities, and educational programs for children and their parents. In addition to its winter season at the Dorothy Chandler Pavilion, the orchestra has made its summer home at the world famous Hollywood Bowl, since 1922, where it plays to huge and appreciative audiences each year. The orchestra has performed with Luciano Pavarotti at the Hollywood Bowl several times.

The Los Angeles Philharmonic has a distinguished touring history, playing in cities across the United States and around the world for nearly forty years. In August 1992, it became the first American orchestra in residence for both opera and concerts at the Salzburg Festival, winning international acclaim for its performances of Messiaen's monumental opera *Saint François d'Assise*, in a new production led by Maestro Salonen and directed by the orchestra's creative consultant, Peter Sellars. More recently, the orchestra was in residence at the Lucerne Easter Festival (1993), and in March of 1994 they toured Taiwan and Japan. Salonen and the Philharmonic returned to Europe in the summer of 1994 and toured the major music festivals.

Los Angeles has traditionally been associated with tremors, not tenors. Indeed, until 1986, the city had the dubious distinction of being the last major population center in the United States without its own large-scale opera company. In its first eight seasons, however, the Los Angeles Music Center Opera—known informally as the L.A. Opera—has proven that the city provides as hospitable a climate for Verdi as it does for verdant lawns.

In 1984, after two decades of importing other companies to the Dorothy Chandler Pavilion, the Music Center Opera Association hired Peter Hemmings to be its first General Director, with the task of creating a company. At the same time, Plácido Domingo became the company's Artistic Consultant, performing there regularly as both a singer and a conductor. The first season in 1986–87 consisted of 21 performances of five operas. For the 1994–95 season, the company presents 54 performances of eight operas.

Among the company's most noteworthy productions are Richard Strauss' *Salome*, directed by Sir Peter Hall and starring Maria Ewing; Wagner's *Tristan und Isolde*, conducted by Zubin Mehta and designed by world-renowned Los Angeles artist David Hockney; and Prokofiev's *The Fiery Angel*, directed by Andrei Serban and designed by Robert Israel.

In 1992, the company hosted the Finnish National Opera in its world première of Aulis Sallinen's *Kullervo*. In 1993, Sir Peter Hall directed a new production of *The Magic Flute*, film director Herbert Ross staged a new production of *La Bohème*, and David Hockney designed Richard Strauss' *Die Frau ohne Schatten*. In January 1994, a rare staging of Manuel Penella's *El Gato Montés* with Justino Díaz, Plácido Domingo and Verónica Villarroel, was videotaped for future international broadcast. The 1994-95 season includes a Peter Sellars production of Debussy's *Pelléas et Mélisande*, new productions of *Porgy and Bess* and *Faust*, and a revival of Verdi's *Otello* with Plácido Domingo and June Anderson.

The L.A. Opera maintains a full program of community activities, including specially commissioned in-school operas, community recitals, and special performances of fully staged operas for student and underserved constituencies.

When the new Disney Hall opens, the L.A. Opera will become the primary tenants of the Dorothy Chandler Pavilion, expecting to fill the hall for 100 performances a year. With the interest of a growing audience, the strength of a vital board of directors, and the support of the company's Founding Angels, led by Warner W. Henry, the L.A. Opera looks to the future with tremendous optimism.

~ THE TRANSFORMATION ~

To take the best advantage of Dodger Stadium's architecture, Tibor Rudas conceived of a plan to place the stage between the embracing arms of the grandstand pavilions, transforming the baseball stadium into a 56,000-seat amphitheater. The result of this planning was an elegant setting recalling the architectural grandeur of classical antiquity.

The rear and sides of the stage were open,
revealing a verdant backdrop and two towering water
cascades. The "forest" was not only decorative
but also functioned as an acoustic shell. The playing
field was covered with a four-level seating area
similar to that found in concert halls but never before
attempted in a sports venue, providing the
audience with unobstructed views.

❧

It took six days of strenuous round-the-clock effort
by hundreds of craftsmen and stagehands to
build this ambitious project. 75 trailer trucks were
needed to deliver the scenic elements and construction
materials to the site.

Lighting the setting was the biggest technical
challenge, since there could be no lighting
towers blocking the audience's view. The problem
was conquered with the innovative use of
state-of-the-art equipment.

❦

Artisans from three continents collaborated
on the massive undertaking. The stage roof, podium,
and risers were designed and built in Australia.
The twenty soaring columns designed by Lázló Székely
were constructed in Hungary. The forest –
one tenth of a mile from end to end and five stories
high – was fabricated in Los Angeles.
The overall scenic design was created by American
art director René Lagler.

The superb sound quality was the result of a computer-designed system which provided acoustical enhancement of the voices and orchestra. Specifically developed for this occasion, its sophisticated design maintained opera house quality for the huge audience. Unlike a public-address system, which projects the sound into the far reaches of the stadium simply by making the music louder, this special equipment took the acoustical properties of the site into account and reinforced the sound where it was needed.

Dodger Stadium was ideal for this event because of its unique shape: the area behind the stage is open, allowing the sound a natural means of escape rather than containing it, only to reverberate unpleasantly within. The sound designers studied the stadium's acoustics for a year in order to guarantee what was without a doubt the finest concert sound ever experienced out-of-doors.

*During the first rehearsal at Pasadena's Civic
Auditorium, the earnest business of music-making
was enlivened by high spirits and horseplay.*

～

*The good-natured comraderie continued as
the artists settled in at Dodger Stadium rehearsals
later in the week.*

～

Two nights before the actual concert, all systems (human and technical) were tested during a full-length rehearsal. Based on the theory that an uneven final rehearsal predicts a strong performance, the upcoming concert was bound to be powerful!

On the day of the concert, every aspect of the
immense undertaking was checked and checked again
to insure that it would proceed without a hitch.

Everything was in place as the late afternoon sun
began to slip down behind the stadium walls.
Eager with anticipation, early arrivals began to
take their seats in the audience even as the
technicians were making their final adjustments.

~

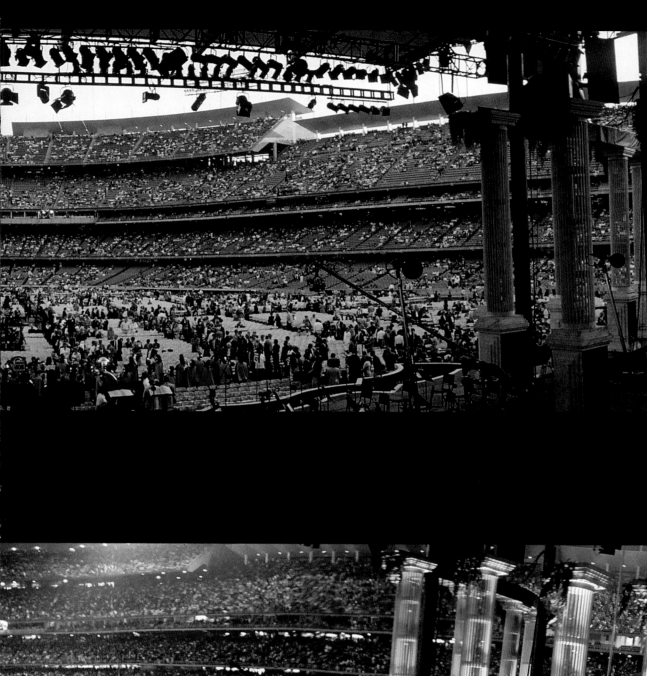

At precisely 8:00 p.m., more than 100 television networks around the world received the satellite feeds as Maestro Mehta strode to the podium. His crisp downbeat propelled the orchestra into the National Anthem of the United States of America.

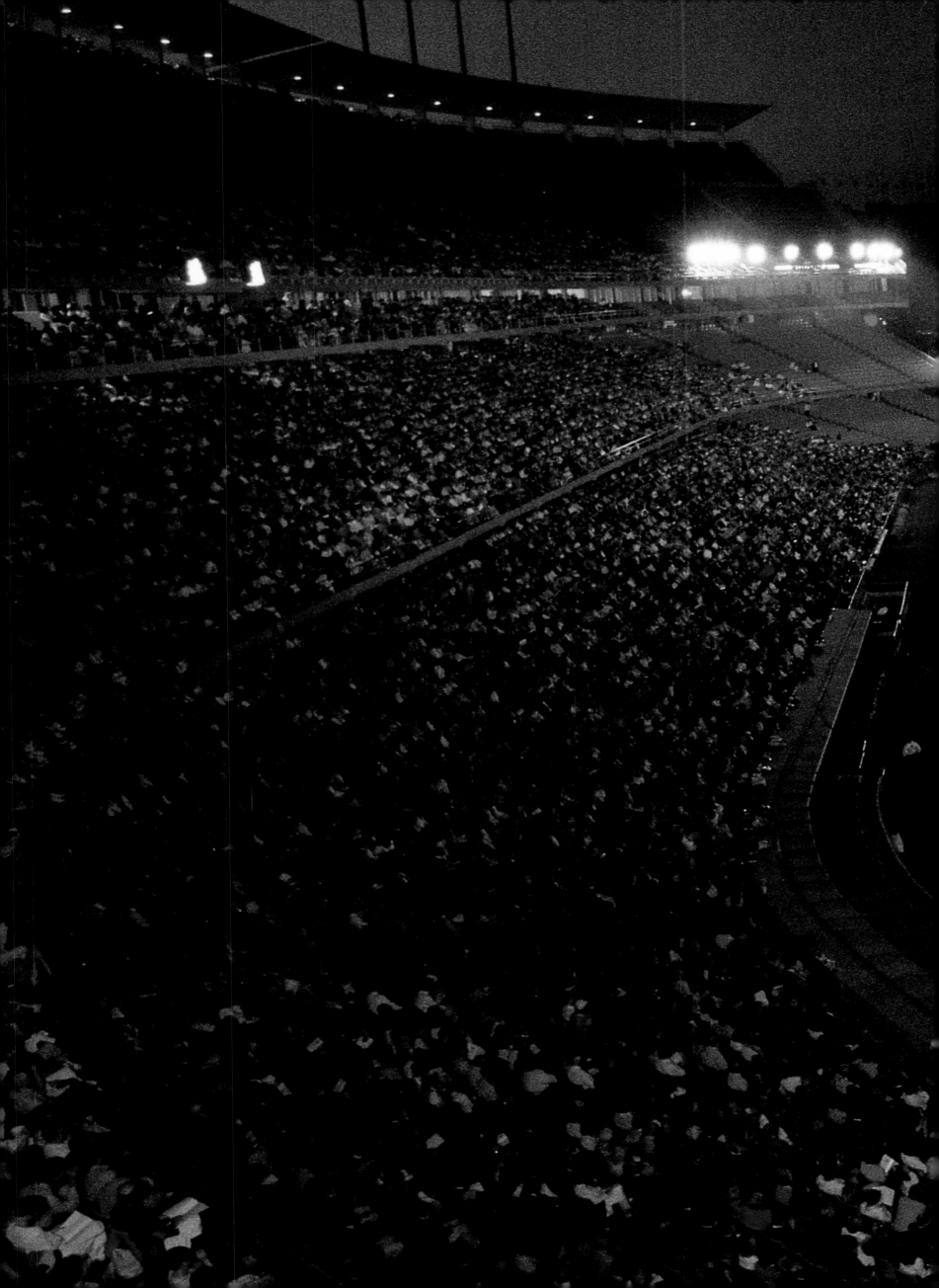

~ THE PERFORMANCE ~

"When each one does his aria, it is all very serious,"
says Maestro Mehta. "But when these three guys
get on stage together, that's when the sparks fly!"

*"And yet even though there is the playful
spirit of mock competition, under it all is a
tremendous respect for each other's talent."*

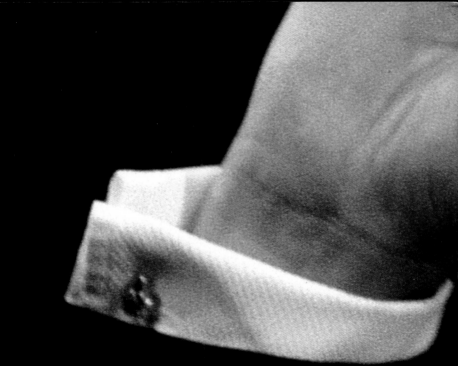

~THE PROGRAM~

OVERTURE
From "CANDIDE"
Music by LEONARD BERNSTEIN

~

Ô SOUVERAIN! Ô JUGE! Ô PÈRE!
From "LE CID"
Music by JULES MASSENET
Text by ADOLPHE D'ENNERY, LOUIS GALLET, and EDOUARD BLAU
Performed by JOSÉ CARRERAS

~

QUANDO LE SERE AL PLACIDO
From "LUISA MILLER"
Music by GIUSEPPE VERDI
Text by SALVATORE CAMMARANO
Performed by PLÁCIDO DOMINGO

~

PORQUOI ME RÉVEILLER
From "WERTHER"
Music by JULES MASSENET
Text by EDOUARD BLAU, PAUL MILLIET
AND GEORGES HARTMANN
Performed by LUCIANO PAVAROTTI

~

WITH A SONG IN MY HEART
From "SPRING IS HERE"
Music by RICHARD RODGERS Text by LORENZ HART
Performed by JOSÉ CARRERAS

~

GRANADA
Music by AGUSTÍN LARA
Performed by PLÁCIDO DOMINGO

~

NON TI SCORDAR DI ME
Music by ERNESTO DE CURTIS
Text by DOMENICO FURNÒ
Performed by LUCIANO PAVAROTTI

~

MEDLEY
A TRIBUTE TO HOLLYWOOD
MY WAY Music by CLAUDE FRANÇOIS and JACQUES REVAUX Text by PAUL ANKA
MOON RIVER Music by HENRY MANCINI Text by JOHNNY MERCER
BECAUSE Music by GUY D'HARDELOT Text by EDWARD TESCHEMACHER
SINGIN' IN THE RAIN Music by NACIO HERB BROWN Text by ARTHUR FREED
Performed by JOSÉ CARRERAS, PLÁCIDO DOMINGO, and LUCIANO PAVAROTTI
Medley arranged and orchestrated by LALO SCHIFRIN

~

HUNGARIAN MARCH
From "THE DAMNATION OF FAUST"
Music by HECTOR BERLIOZ

~

TU, CA NUN CHIAGNE
Music by ERNESTO DE CURTIS
Text by LIBERO BOVIO
Performed by JOSÉ CARRERAS

~

AMOR, VIDA DE MI VIDA
From "MARAVILLA"
Music by FEDERICO MORENO TORROBA
Text by ANTONIO QUINTERO and JESÚS MARIA DE AROZAMENA
Performed by PLÁCIDO DOMINGO

∼

AVE MARIA
Music by FRANZ SCHUBERT
Based on a poem by SIR WALTER SCOTT
Performed by LUCIANO PAVAROTTI

∼

E LUCEVAN LE STELLE
From "TOSCA"
Music by GIACOMO PUCCINI
Text by GIUSEPPE GIACOSA and LUIGI ILLICA
Performed by JOSÉ CARRERAS

∼

VESTI LA GIUBBA
From "PAGLIACCI"
Music and text by RUGGIERO LEONCAVALLO
Performed by PLÁCIDO DOMINGO

∼

NESSUN DORMA!
From "TURANDOT"
Music by GIACOMO PUCCINI
Text by GIUSEPPE ADAMI and RENATE SIMONI
Performed by LUCIANO PAVAROTTI

∼

MEDLEY
AROUND THE WORLD
AMERICA From "WEST SIDE STORY" Music by LEONARD BERNSTEIN Text by STEPHEN SONDHEIM
ALL I ASK OF YOU From "THE PHANTOM OF THE OPERA"
Music by ANDREW LLOYD WEBBER Text by CHARLES HART
Additional text by RICHARD STILGOE
FUNICULÌ, FUNICULÀ Music by LUIGI DENZA Text by TURCO AND ZANDARINI
SOUS LES PONTS DE PARIS Music by VINCENT SCOTTO
English Text by DORCAS COCHRAN French Text by J. RODOR
BRAZIL Music by ARY BARROSO English Text by S.K. RUSSELL
BE MY LOVE From "THE TOAST OF NEW ORLEANS"
Music by NICHOLAS BRODSZKY Text by SAMMY CAHN
MARECHIARE Music by FRANCESCO PAOLO TOSTI Text by SALVATORE DI GIACOMO
LIPPEN SCHWEIGEN From "THE MERRY WIDOW" Music by FRANZ LEHÁR
Text by VICTOR LÉON and LEO STEIN
SANTA LUCIA LUNTANA Music and text by GIOVANNI MATTEO MARIO
THOSE WERE THE DAYS Music and text by GENE RASKIN
TE QUIERO DIJISTE Music and text by MARIA GREVER
TORNA A SURRIENTO Music and text by ERNESTO DE CURTIS
Performed by JOSÉ CARRERAS, PLÁCIDO DOMINGO, and LUCIANO PAVAROTTI
Medley arranged and orchestrated by LALO SCHIFRIN

∼

ENCORE
LA DONNA É MOBILE
From "RIGOLETTO" Music by GUISEPPE VERDI Text by FRANCESCO MARIA PIAVE
Based on the play "Le Roi s'amuse" by Victor Hugo
LIBIAMO, NE'LIETI CALICI ("BRINDISI")
From "LA TRAVIATA" Music by GIUSEPPE VERDI Text by FRANCESCO MARIA PIAVE
Based on the play "Le Dame aux Camélias" by Alexandre Dumas fils

∼

Ô SOUVERAIN! Ô JUGE! Ô PÈRE!

"El Cid" was Rodrigo Díaz de Vivar (in Arabic, *El Seid*—"The Conqueror"), a legendary nobleman who lived during the Moorish occupation of Spain (1043–1099 A.D.). Murder, political intrigue, and charges of treason have taken their toll and left him stripped of everything but courage. Alone and despondent in his tent on the eve of war, he laments his separation from his beloved Chimène. Far outnumbered by the opposing armies, he fears certain defeat in the coming battle. This heartfelt prayer affirms his profound faith in the Almighty, faith soon rewarded when a vision of Saint James appears to him, assuring victory.

Few details about the actual man exist. His real life, like that of most legends, seems to have been somewhat less sensational than his press. Nevertheless, tales of his reputation for courage and mercy soon found their way into the popular literature of the age. Nearly a millenium after his death, the legend of El Cid has been refreshed in our own time by the film starring America's "epic hero," Charlton Heston, with Sophia Loren as Chimène.

From "LE CID" Music by JULES MASSENET (1842–1912)
Text by ADOLPHE D'ENNERY, LOUIS GALLET,
and EDOUARD BLAU

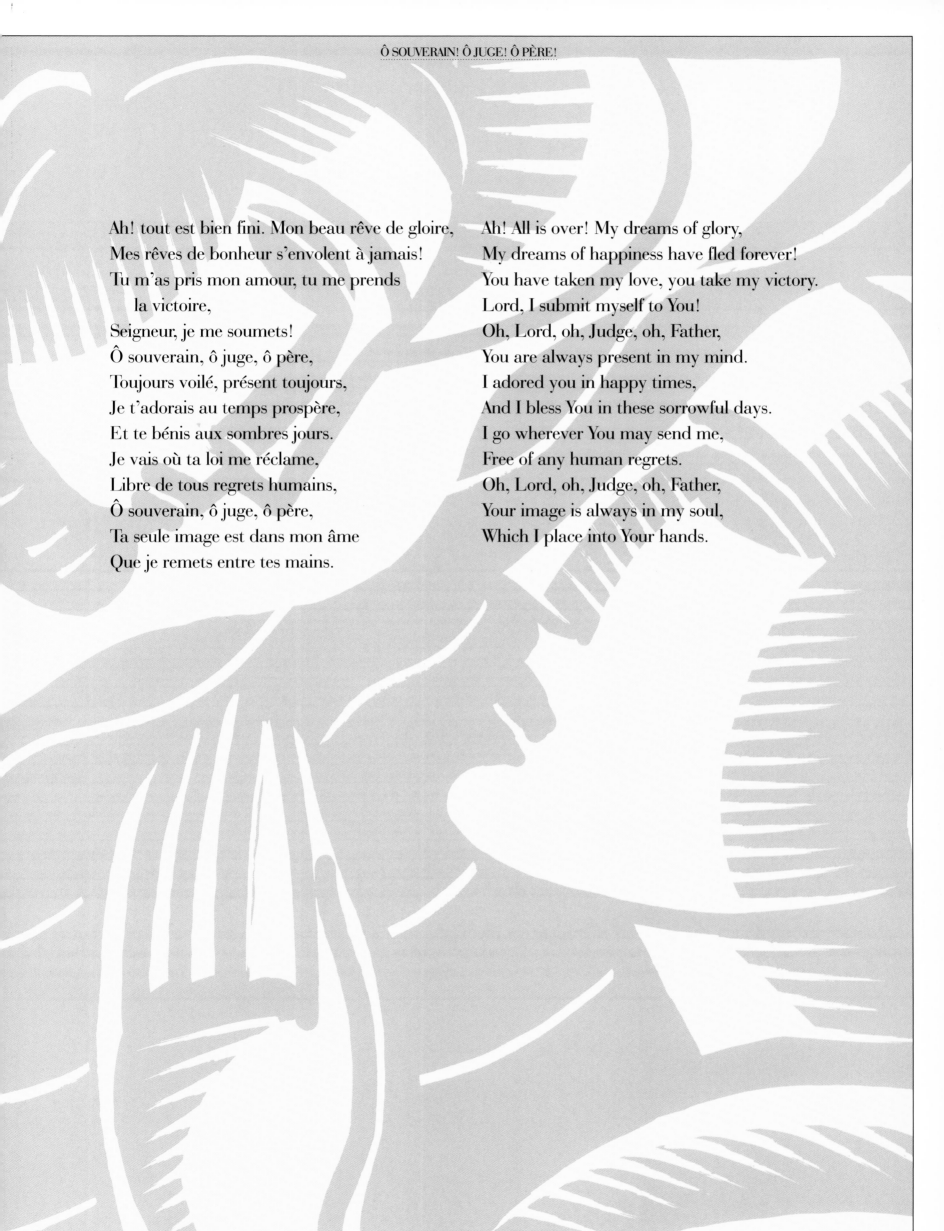

Ah! tout est bien fini. Mon beau rêve de gloire,
Mes rêves de bonheur s'envolent à jamais!
Tu m'as pris mon amour, tu me prends
　　la victoire,
Seigneur, je me soumets!
Ô souverain, ô juge, ô père,
Toujours voilé, présent toujours,
Je t'adorais au temps prospère,
Et te bénis aux sombres jours.
Je vais où ta loi me réclame,
Libre de tous regrets humains,
Ô souverain, ô juge, ô père,
Ta seule image est dans mon âme
Que je remets entre tes mains.

Ah! All is over! My dreams of glory,
My dreams of happiness have fled forever!
You have taken my love, you take my victory.
Lord, I submit myself to You!
Oh, Lord, oh, Judge, oh, Father,
You are always present in my mind.
I adored you in happy times,
And I bless You in these sorrowful days.
I go wherever You may send me,
Free of any human regrets.
Oh, Lord, oh, Judge, oh, Father,
Your image is always in my soul,
Which I place into Your hands.

QUANDO LE SERE AL PLACIDO

Love, honor and jealousy are the passions that so often propel the characters in opera. In *Luisa Miller*, Verdi arranges them in a fateful triangle, straining the loyalties of parents and children and the bonds of trust between lovers.

The story takes place in a Tyrolean village in the early eighteenth century. Luisa and Rodolfo are in love. She is the daughter of a retired soldier. He is the noble son of Count Walter, disguised as a peasant. To make matters more complicated, Luisa has agreed to marry the Count's conniving steward, (whose name "Wurm" speaks volumes about his character). And Rodolfo has been promised by his father to a wealthy widow.

Enraged when he learns that his son loves the common Luisa, the Count imprisons her father. To save the old man's life, Luisa writes a letter to Rodolfo denying her love for him. Just as the Count and Wurm have planned, the letter falls into Rodolfo's hands. More devastated than his father could have imagined, Rodolfo resolves to kill both Luisa and himself.

Verdi's exquisite music underscores the plot as it dramatically unfolds toward its inevitable, tragic end — never more beautifully than in this aria in which Rodolfo laments his apparent betrayal.

From "LUISA MILLER"
Music by GIUSEPPE VERDI (1813 - 1901)
Text by SALVATORE CAMMARANO

Oh! fede negar potessi agl'occhi miei!
Se cielo e terra, se mortali ed angeli
attestarmi volesser ch'ella non è rea,
mentite! io responder dovrei, tutti mentite.

Son cifre sue! Tanta perfidia! Un'alma
sì nera! sì mendace!
Ben la conobbe il padre!
Ma dunque i giuri, le speranze, la gioia,
le lagrime, l'affanno?
Tutto è menzogna, tradimento, inganno!

Quando le sere al placido
chiaror d'un ciel stellato
meco figgea nell'etere
lo sguardo innamorato,
e questa mano stringermi
dalla sua man sentia...
ah! mi tradia!
Allor, ch'io muto, estatico
da'labbri suoi pendea,
ed alla in suon angelico,
"amo te sol" dicea,
tal che sembrò l'empireo
apirsi all'alma mia!
Ah! mi tradia!

Oh, if only I could deny trust in my very eyes!
If heaven and earth, if mortals and angels
were to reassure me that she is not guilty,
I should have to reply: you all lie!

This is her writing! Such treachery! A heart
so black, so false!
My father knew her well!
But what of the vows, the hopes, the joy,
the tears, the anguish?
All is falsehood, betrayal, deception!

When at eventide, in the tranquil
glimmer of a starry sky,
with me she gazed lovingly
into space
and I felt this hand of mine
pressed by hers...
Ah! She betrayed me.
Then I, silent, ecstatic,
would hang onto her words
when she in angelic tones said:
"I love you, I love only you,"
so that paradise seemed
to open to my soul!
Ah, she betrayed me!

PORQUOI ME REVELLER

It is autumn in late-19th century Frankfurt, and Charlotte has married Albert in order to keep a promise she made to her dying mother. At the wedding, she begs the young romantic dreamer, Werther, who is deeply in love with her, to leave the city rather than persist with his constant and passionate attentions. When they are reunited weeks later on Christmas Eve, she knows it is Werther she truly loves in spite of her efforts to repress her feelings toward him. Together again, they are reminded of the happy memories of shared moments of beauty in their lives. Opening one of the many books they once enjoyed together, he reads to her this sad lament from the poetry of Ossian, which perfectly expresses the futility of their love.

Massenet based his opera on "The Sorrows of Young Werther," an immensely popular novel which captured the essential spirit of the Romantic Age.

From "WERTHER"
Music by JULES MASSENET (1842 – 1912)
Text by EDOUARD BLAU, PAUL MILLIET AND
GEORGES HARTMANN

Pourquoi me réveiller, ô souffle du printemps?
Sur mon front je sens tes caresses,
et pourtant bien proche est le temps
des orages et des tristesses!
Pourquoi me réveiller, ô souffle du printemps?
Demain, dans le vallon, viendra le voyageur,
se souvenant de ma gloire première,
et ses yeuz vainement chercheront ma splen-
deur:
ils ne trouveront plus que deuil et que misère!
Hélas! Pourquoi me réveiller, ô souffle du
printemps?

Why awaken me, O breath of spring?
On my brow I feel thy caresses,
and yet the time of storms
and of sorrows is nigh!
Why awaken me, O breath of spring?
Tomorrow the traveller will come into the dale
recalling my former glory,
and in vain will his eyes seek my splendor:
they will find naught but mourning and
despair!
Alas! Why awaken me, O breath of spring?

WITH A SONG IN MY HEART

Mario Lanza, one of the most charismatic singers of his generation, motivated millions of fans to imitate his vocal style (if only in the shower!). He became the first "crossover" star to bridge the classical and popular repertoire, becoming RCA's top-selling recording artist in the process. Lanza's portrayal of an equally celebrated tenor in the film *The Great Caruso* (1951) inspired many of his admirers—including Mr. Carreras—to pursue serious musical careers. Lanza made a total of five films for MGM, all of them featuring remarkably popular renditions of operatic highlights.

With a Song In My Heart, one of Mario Lanza's favorites, was originally written for the Broadway show *Spring is Here* in 1929. It became a popular hit in 1952 as the title song of an inspiring biography. In the Oscar-winning film, Susan Hayward portrays Jane Froman, the popular American singer of the 30's, who makes a remarkable recovery after serious injuries sustained in a plane crash nearly ended her career.

From "SPRING IS HERE"
Music by RICHARD RODGERS (1902–1979)
Text by LORENZ HART

With a song in my heart.
I behold your adorable face,
Just a song at the start,
But it soon is a hymn to your grace.
When the music swells
I'm touching your hand;
It tells that you're standing near, and
At the sound of your voice
Heaven opens its portals to me.
Can I help but rejoice
That a song such as ours came to be?
But I always knew
I would live life through
With a song in my heart for you.

GRANADA

Granada is an exotic and magical place. Commanding the foothills of the Sierra Nevada mountains of southern Spain, it was the final stronghold of the Moors who occupied the Iberian Peninsula for seven centuries. Granada's history is enriched by its numerous contributions to art, literature and science. Its cathedral is the final resting place of Ferdinand and Isabel, the first rulers of a united Spain, who sent Columbus on his fateful journey westward.

The wondrous lore of this ancient capital is laden with tales of romance and adventure, inspired in part by the beautiful Moorish architecture and gardens of the Alhambra palace which dominate the cliffs above the city.

Granada's allure certainly inspired the romantic instincts of Agustín Lara, a remarkably prolific Mexican composer. He wrote more than 600 songs including "Maria Bonita" and "Solamente Una Vez."

Music and Spanish lyric by AGUSTÍN LARA (1900-1970)

Granada, tierra soñada por mí,
mi cantar se vuelve gitano
cuando es para ti.
Mi cantar, hecho de fantasía,
mi cantar, flor de melancolía,
que yo te vengo a dar.
Granada, tierra ensangrentada
en tardes de toros,
mujer que conserva el embrujo
de los ojos moros.
De sueño, rebelde, gitana
cubierta de flores,
y beso tu boca de grana,
jugosa manzana
que me habla de amores.
Granada, manola, cantada
en coplas preciosas,
no tengo otra cosa que darte
que un ramo de rosas,
de rosas de suave fragrancia
que le dieran marco
a la Virgen morena.
Granada, tu tierra está llena
de lindas mujeres, de sangre
y de sol.

Granada, I'm falling under your spell.
And if you could speak,
what a fascinating tale you would tell —
of an age the world has long forgotten,
of an age that weaves
a silent magic in Granada today.
The dawn in the sky greets the day
with a sigh for Granada,
For she can remember the splendor
that once was Granada.
It still can be found
in the hills all around
as I wander along,
entranced by a land
full of sunshine and flowers and song.
And soon it will welcome the stars,
while guitars play a soft habanera;
then moonlit Granada will live again
the glory of yesterday,
romantic and gay.
And when day is done
and the sun starts
to set in Granada
I envy the blush of the snowclad
Sierra Nevada.

NON TI SCORDAR DI ME

The Neapolitan song evolved during the last years of the 19th century in the sunshine of Italy's Mediterranean port city Naples, where literally thousands of melodies were written by dozens of composers. The greatest of the songwriters, including Tosti, Bixio and de Curtis, attained a perfect match of voice, artistic temperament and poetry rarely achieved in music. Their music found willing performers in the singers there, who filled the air with their evocative refrains.

Hearing them again prompts memories of long ago afternoons spent listening to these songs around the phonograph. Their lilting melodies were beloved by Gigli, di Stefano, Caruso, and many other singers whose recordings from an earlier age have become part of a lasting vocal tradition. These ballads continue to be passed along affectionately from generation to generation, and not surprisingly, each of the three tenors has recorded several albums with his own particular favorites from this repertoire.

Music by ERNESTO DE CURTIS (1863–1945)

Text by DOMENICO FURNÒ

Partirono le rondini dal mio paese freddo
   e senza sole,
Cercando primavere di viole,
Nidi d'amore e di felicità.
La mia piccola rondine partì
Senza lasciarmi un bacio,
Senza un addio partì.

Non ti scordar di me:
La vita mia legata è a te.
Io t'amo sempre più,
Nel sogno mio rimani tu.
Non ti scordar di me:
La vita mia legata è a te.
C'è sempre un nido
   nel mio cor per te.
Non ti scordar di me!

The swallows flew away from my cold
   and sunless land,
in search of spring and violets,
nests of love and happiness.
My little swallow flew away
without a kiss,
with no farewell she left.

Do not forget me:
my life is bound up in you.
I love you more and more,
my dreams are always of you.
Do not forget me:
my life is bound up in you.
There will always be a nest
   in my heart for you.
Do not forget me!

TU, CA NUN CHIAGNE

Traditionally, Neapolitan songs were performed to the music of the mandolin, guitar, or accordian, their verses sometimes going on and on to tell a complicated tale. Some are lighthearted serenades from sleepless lovers, others passionate laments by melancholy youths, but all of them are poems that capture the intimacy of friendship, the profound nature of desire, and a passionate love of nature. And above all, they are a true and intimate reflection of the Neapolitan soul.

Even though Enrico Caruso, who was born in Naples, was responsible perhaps more than anyone else for popularizing these wonderful songs, you don't have to be Neapolitan—or even Italian—to sing them. Great tenors from around Italy and the world have added to their fame. Gigli came from Ricanti in central Italy, Schipa was from Lecce in the south, di Stefano was from Sicily, and Mario Lanza was from South Philadelphia. Over the years, many of these songs have become classics, including this one, whose singer is overwhelmed with desire for an absent love.

Music by ERNESTO DE CURTIS (1863–1945)
Text by LIBERO BOVIO

Comm'è bella a muntagna stanotte…
bella accussì nun l'aggio vista maie!
'N'anema pare rassignata e stanca
sotto cuperta 'e chesta lune janca…

Tu che nun chiagne e chiagnere me faie,
tu, stanotte addò staie?
Voglio a te!
Voglio a te!
Chist' uocchie te vonno
n'ata vota vedè!

Commè calma 'a muntagna stanotte…
cchiù calma 'e mo nun l'aggio vista maie!
E tutto dorme, tutto dorme o more,
e i sulo veglio, perchè veglia Ammore…

Tu che nun chiagne e chiagnere me faie,
tu, stanotte addò staie?
Voglio a te!
Voglio a te!
Chist' uocchie te vonno
n'ata vota vedè!

How beautiful the mountain is tonight…
it has never looked this beautiful before!
It seems to be a soul, resigned and weary
beneath the candid coverlet of the moon…

You who weep not while you make me weep,
where are you tonight?
I need you!
I need you!
These eyes of mine desire
to see you once more!

How calm and quiet the mountain is tonight…
I've never seen it calm like this before!
All is asleep, all is asleep or dying,
I watch alone, for Love is watching too…

You who weep not while you make me weep,
where are you tonight?
I need you!
I need you!
These eyes of mine desire
to see you once more!

AMOR, VIDA DE MI VIDA

Zarzuela, the Spanish equivalent of Viennese operetta and Italian opera buffa, traces its roots to the 17th century. La Zarzuela, a royal hunting lodge on the outskirts of Madrid, had been converted by the 29-year-old king Philip IV into an elaborately decorated retreat. For his amusement, *fiestas de Zarzuela*, short comedies with music and singing, were devised. Spain's leading writers of the time collaborated on zarzuelas with more serious-minded subjects, but even those works maintained the popular touch; scenes with shepherds and shepherdesses singing *seguidillas* were interspersed with those of Greek gods in conversation.

While the early works bear little resemblance to the literally thousands of melodramatic and sentimental pieces which came to be popular by the turn of the last century, all zarzuelas share an intrinsically Spanish form and style. Moreno Torroba wrote more than 100 works, including the classic zarzuelas *Luisa Fernanda* and *La Chulapona*.

From "MARAVILLA"
Music by FEDERICO MORENO TORROBA (1891–1982)
Text by ANTONIO QUINTERO
and JESÚS MARIA DE AROZAMENA

Adiós, dijiste:
se va mi vida.
Llorar quisiste
por un amor que hay
que olvidar.
Te vas riendo
¡y yo me muero!
Mi dolor es saber
que no puedes llorar.

Amor, vida de mi vida,
¡qué triste es decirse adiós!
Te llevas la juventud
de éste querer sin redención,
amor que por el camino
no puedes volver atrás.
Te ríes cuando sientes
deseos de llorar.

Y pensar que te amé
con alma y vida,
y hoy te quieres
burlar de mi dolor.
Este amor que soñé
no lo puedo callar.
Fueron falsas palabras,
mentistes mil veces
tu amor, mujer.

Amor, vida de mi vida, *etc*.

¡Adiós, mi bien!
¡Ah, adiós!

You said farewell:
my life is departing.
You wished to weep
for a love
that must be forgotten.
You go, laughing,
and I am dying!
My sorrow is to know
that you cannot weep.

Love, life of my life,
how sad it is to say good-bye!
Youth deprives you
of this love, without redemption,
love that you cannot turn back
on its path.
You laugh when you feel
a wish to weep.

And to think that I loved you
with my body and soul,
and now you wish
to mock me in my grief.
I cannot suppress this love
of which I dreamed.
Your words of love
were false, woman:
you lied a thousand times.

Love, life of my life, *etc*.

Farewell, my love!
Ah, farewell!

AVE MARIA

Franz Schubert in his short life was one of history's most prolific and original composers, and one with a genius for melody. Sir Walter Scott's narrative poem, *The Lady of the Lake*, inspired this hymn to the Virgin. It is among Schubert's last and most beautiful compositions. Scott's poem includes the words of the Latin prayer, *Ave Maria*, which has been used in devotions since the 11th century. The text is based on the greeting of the angel Gabriel to Mary (St. Luke 1:28, 1:42), announcing her as the mother of Jesus. This prayer has often been set to music, but never in a lovelier way.

Gioacchino Rossini, composer of *The Barber of Seville* and many other popular operas, also found inspiration in this Scottish epic and created the opera *La Donna del Lago* from its poetic lines. Scott's other romantic ballads and novels on Scottish history provided the basis for many musical works, particularly Donizetti's opera, *Lucia di Lammermoor.*

Music by FRANZ SCHUBERT (1797–1828)
Based on a poem by SIR WALTER SCOTT (1771–1832)

Ave Maria!
Vergin del ciel,
sovrana di grazie e madre pia,
accogli ognor la fervente preghiera,
non negar a questo smarrito mio cor
tregua nel suo dolor!
Sprduta l'alma mia ricorre a te,
e piena di speme si prostra ai tuoi pié,
t'implor' e attende la bella pace
che solo tu le puoi donar.
Ave Maria!

Ave Maria!
Gratia plena,
Maria, gratia plena *etc*.
Ave, ave, Dominus tecum.
Benedicta tu in mulieribus,
et benedictus,
et benedictus fructus ventris
tui, Jesu.
Ave Maria!

Hail Mary!
Virgin of heaven,
queen of grace and holy mother,
receive a fervent prayer,
do not deny my bewildered heart
relief in its distress!
My lost soul turns to you,
and at your feet, full of hope,
implores you and awaits the sweet peace
that only you can give.
Hail Mary!

Hail Mary!
Full of grace,
Mary, full of grace *etc*.
Hail, hail, the Lord is with thee.
Blessed art thou among women,
and blessed,
blessed is the fruit of
thy womb, Jesus.
Hail Mary!

E LUCEVAN LE STELLE

It is June, 1800, and political turmoil permeates the sweltering air of the Roman summer. Bonaparte is on the march against Italy. The Roman despots have filled the detested prison of Castel Sant'Angelo with patriotic sympathizers clamoring for a Republic. The painter Mario Cavaradossi is among them, not only for aiding the cause against tyranny, but also for loving the enchanting Floria Tosca, a tempestuous and dazzlingly beautiful star of the opera. Tosca has been horrified by the lecherous advances of Baron Scarpia, the hypocritically pious chief of the Roman police. Scarpia will go to any lengths to crush the political opposition. He cruelly coerces Tosca to betray Cavaradossi, who now sits alone in his cell awaiting the dawn — and his execution.

As the faint light of morning tints the sky and the sweet song of a shepherd boy joins the tolling of distant church bells, Cavaradossi composes a final letter to his beloved. Facing death, and never more in love with life, he is overwhelmed by his memories of Tosca.

From "TOSCA"
Music by GIACOMO PUCCINI (1858 - 1924)
Text by LUIGI ILLICA and GIUSEPPE GIACOSA

E lucevan le stelle
ed olezzava la terra,

stridea l'uscio dell'orto,
e un passo sfiorava la rena...
Entrava ella, fragrante,
Mi cadea fra le braccia...
Oh, dolci baci, o languide carezze,
Mentr'io fremente
Le belle forme disciogliea dai veli!
Svan" per sempre il sogno mio d'amore...
L'ora è fuggita...
E muoio disperato!
E non ho amato mai tanto la vita!

And the stars shone
and the earth was perfumed.

The gate to the garden creaked
And a footstep rustled the sand to the path...
Fragrant, she entered
and fell into my arms...
Oh soft kisses, oh sweet abandon,
as I trembling unloosed her veils and
disclosed her beauty!
Oh vanished forever is that dream of love,
Fled is that hour...
and I desperately die.
And never before have I loved life so much!

VESTI LA GIUBBA

Canio, an actor in a troupe of strolling players, is preparing backstage for the evening's performance. Embittered by the knowledge that he has been betrayed by the woman he loves, he sings this poignant lament. It reveals the agony of a man who is paid to play the clown, but who suffers personal tragedy privately in silence. The theme is timeless, and the music perfectly captures its essence in one of the most famous songs in opera.

Opera is full of tales of gods and heroes, but hardly ever stories about the people next door. *Pagliacci* is an opera, along with *Cavalleria Rusticana*, with which it is often paired, that set a standard for the turn-of-the-century *verismo* tradition. In this style of opera, the action concerns the "realistic" true-life dramas of ordinary people and their passions. Canio is among the most taxing and emotionally draining roles in that repertoire, challenging all of the tenor's skills and resources.

From "PAGLIACCI"
Music and text by RUGGIERO LEONCAVALLO
(1858–1919)

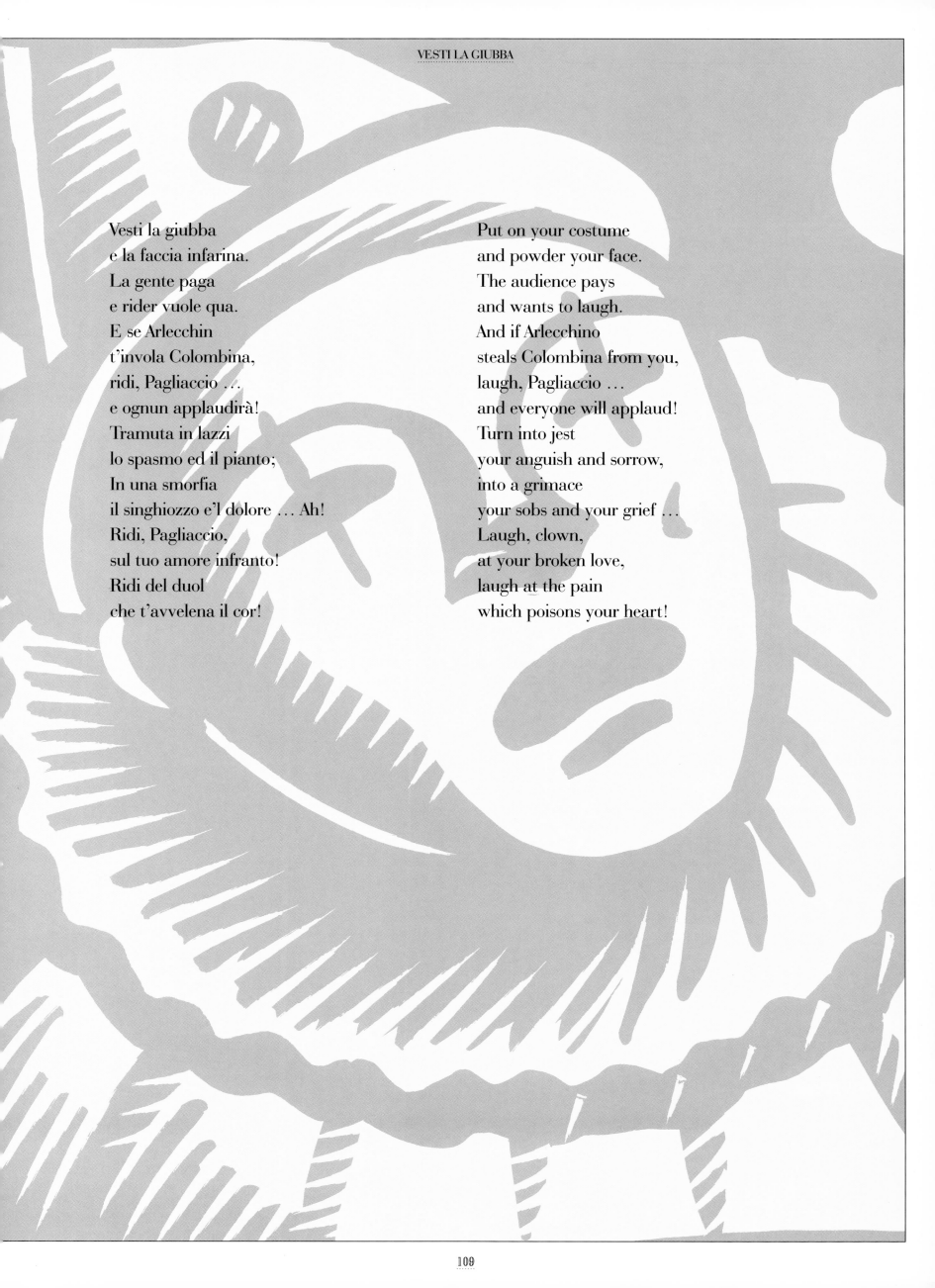

Vesti la giubba
e la faccia infarina.
La gente paga
e rider vuole qua.
E se Arlecchin
t'invola Colombina,
ridi, Pagliaccio …
e ognun applaudirà!
Tramuta in lazzi
lo spasmo ed il pianto;
In una smorfia
il singhiozzo e'l dolore … Ah!
Ridi, Pagliaccio,
sul tuo amore infranto!
Ridi del duol
che t'avvelena il cor!

Put on your costume
and powder your face.
The audience pays
and wants to laugh.
And if Arlecchino
steals Colombina from you,
laugh, Pagliaccio …
and everyone will applaud!
Turn into jest
your anguish and sorrow,
into a grimace
your sobs and your grief …
Laugh, clown,
at your broken love,
laugh at the pain
which poisons your heart!

NESSUN DORMA!

Legendary China is the setting of this exotic fable. The beautiful and cruel princess Turandot has sworn to avenge her ancient ancestor, Princess Lou-Ling, who was murdered by an invader. Turandot promises her hand in marriage to the one who can solve her three inscrutable riddles, but death to he who fails. Although many before him have perished, a mysterious prince has fearlessly challenged Turandot and answered the questions correctly. She must now submit to his love, but the prince tells her that if she can discover his name by sunrise, he will forfeit his life. In this aria, he eagerly awaits the dawn and the victory of love, musing that no one in Peking will sleep while Turandot seeks his name, which he alone knows.

Puccini found the inspiration for this work in a fable by the eighteenth-century Venetian playwright Carlo Gozzi, fascinated by the possibilities of exploring the nature of "Turandot's amorous passion, which she has smothered so long beneath the ashes of her great pride."

From "TURANDOT"
Music by GIACOMO PUCCINI (1858–1924)
Text by GIUSEPPE ADAMI and RENATO SIMONI

Nessun dorma! Nessun dorma!
Tu pure, o Principessa,
nella tua fredda stanza
guardi le stelle che tremano
d'amore e di speranza!
Ma il mio mistero è chiuso in me,
il nome mio nessun saprà!
No, no, sulla tua bocca lo dirò,
cuando la luce splenderà!
Ed il mio bacio scioglierà
il silenzio che ti fa mia!

Dilegua, o notte!
Tramontate, stelle!
Tramontate, stelle! All'alba vincerò!
Vincerò! Vincerò!

No man shall sleep! No man shall sleep!
You too, o Princess,
in your chaste room
are watching the stars which
tremble with love and hope!
But my secret lies hidden within me,
no one shall discover my name!
Oh no, I will reveal it only on your lips,
when daylight shines forth
and my kiss shall break
the silence which makes you mine!

Depart, oh night!
Hasten your setting, you stars!
Set, you stars! At dawn I shall win!
I shall win! I shall win!

LA DONNA É MOBILE

Rigoletto, hunchbacked jester to the handsome, lecherous Duke of Mantua, amuses the duke by making caustic fun of everyone else in court. For several months, the Duke has been lusting after an innocent young girl whom he sees only in church. He does not realize, however, that the object of his desire is Rigoletto's own daughter, Gilda.

The Duke's courtiers, who know that Rigoletto visits Gilda secretly every night, think the girl is the hated jester's mistress. With Rigoletto's unwitting assistance, they kidnap her to the palace. Having betrayed his own daughter, and forced to beg for her return, he vows bloody revenge. But Gilda, infatuated with the Duke, pleads with her father to spare his life.

To expose the Duke's real nature to his lovesick daughter, Rigoletto brings her to a rundown inn by the river, home of the harlot Maddalena. Concealed, Gilda observes the Duke with growing horror as he arrives for another amorous adventure, singing this cynical aria. And it is here that the gruesome tragedy of the opera unfolds.

FROM "RIGOLETTO"
MUSIC BY GIUSEPPE VERDI (1813 -- 1901)
TEXT BY FRANCESO MARIA PIAVE
Based on the play "Le Roi s'amuse" by Victor Hugo

La donna è mobile
qual piuma al vento,
muta d'accento
e di pensier.
Sempre un amabile
leggiadro viso,
in pianto o in riso,
è menzogner.

È sempre misero
chi a lei s'affida,
chi le confida
mal cauto il cor!
Pur mai non sentesi
felice appieno
chi su quel seno
non liba amor!

Oh, woman is fickle
as a feather in the wind,
simple in speech,
and simpler in the mind.
Always the lovable,
sweet, laughing face,
but laughing or crying,
a false face, be sure.

Oh, the poor devil,
who gives himself up to her,
and if he trusts her,
there goes his heart!
Yet no man can feel
quite fully content
unless in her arms,
he drinks to love's health!

LIBIAMO, NE' LIETI CALICI ("BRINDISI")

The city is Paris, the year sometime around 1850. It is nearly the end of summer, and the beautiful courtesan Violetta Valéry is giving another glittering party at home. Her current amour, the Baron Douphol, has just arrived with several of their friends. Among them is Gastone, who has brought along Alfredo Germont, a young man who has been eager to make the acquaintance of this captivating hostess. As they dine in candlelit splendor, Gastone tells Violetta that Alfredo had frequently asked about her during her recent illness. She is flattered by Alfredo's attentions, much to the annoyance of the Baron. Gastone proposes a toast, and Alfredo, captivated by Violetta, responds with this spirited song in praise of wine and love.

La Traviata is based on La Dame aux Camélias, a drama by Verdi's contemporary, Alexandre Dumas fils, which in turn reflects the sad history of Dumas' infatuation with a real Parisienne courtesan, Marie Duplessis, who died of consumption in 1847 at the age of 23.

FROM "LA TRAVIATA"
Music by GIUSEPPE VERDI (1813 -- 1901)
Text by FRANCESCO MARIA PIAVE
Based on the play "La Dame aux Camélias" by
Alexandre Dumas fils

Libiamo ne' lieti calici
che la bellezza infiora,
e la fuggevol ora
s'inebrii a voluttà.
Libiam ne' dolci fremiti
che suscita l'amore,
poiché quell'occhio al core
onnipotente va . . .
Libiamo, amore fra I calici
più caldi baci avrà.

Tra voi saprò dividere
il tempo mio giocondo;
tutto è follia nel mondo
ciò che non è piacer.
Godiam, fugace e rapido
è il gaudio dell'amore;
è un fior che nasce e muore,
né più si può goder.
Godiam, c'invita un fervido
accento lusinghier.

(Ah! godiam . . . la tazza e il cantico
la notte abbella e il riso;
in questo paradiso
ne scopra il nuovo dì.)

La vita è nel tripudio
quando non s'ami ancora.
Nol dite a chi l'ignora,
è il mio destin così . . .

Let us drink from the goblets of joy
adorned with beauty,
and the fleeting hour
shall be intoxicated with pleasure.
Let us drink to the secret raptures
which love excites,
for this eye
reigns supreme in my heart . . .
Let us drink, for with wine love
will enjoy yet more passionate kisses.

With you I can spend
the time with delight;
in life everything is folly
which does not bring pleasure.
Let us be happy, fleeting and rapid
is the delight of love;
it is a flower which blooms and dies,
which can no longer be enjoyed.
Let us be happy, fervent
and enticing words summon us.

(Ah! be happy . . . wine and song
and laughter beautify the night;
let the new day find us
in this paradise.)

Life is nothing but pleasure
as long as one is not in love.
Don't say that to one who does not know it.)
That is my fate . . .

~ TRIBUTE ~

In this special "Tribute to Hollywood" medley,
the Three Tenors warmly saluted three other musical immortals.
They sang "My Way" to an approving Frank Sinatra,
"Singing in the Rain" to an appreciative Gene Kelly,
and "Moon River" in memory of the late Henry Mancini,
whose untimely passing a few weeks before the concert was a great
loss to everyone who loves music.

"Vincero!" With the thrilling climax of *Verdi's* Nessun Dorma! *resounding into the night sky, the huge Dodger Stadium audience erupts in a thunderous ovation. The sound made by 56,000 enraptured music-lovers cannot adequately be described in a book, but those who were among them will never forget it.*

The songs and arias of the two showstopping medleys of the 1994 Los Angeles Concert were personally selected by the 3 Tenors and Zubin Mehta. The medleys were then arranged and orchestrated by world-renowned pianist, composer and conductor Lalo Schifrin, who spent nearly five months perfecting these charming and powerful arrangements.

Mr. Schifrin's ability to switch musical gears makes him unique in the music world. He is equally at home conducting or composing for a symphony orchestra, performing at an international jazz festival, or scoring a film or television show. As a jazz musician he has performed and recorded with great personalities such as Dizzy Gillespie, Ella Fitzgerald and Count Basie. His Classical Concertos have been recorded by orchestras such as the London Philharmonic, the Paris Philharmonic and the National Symphony Orchestra.

LALO SCHIFRIN

Born into a musical family, Lalo Schifrin received classical training in music, and also studied law in his native Argentina. He continued his formal music education at the Paris Conservatory during the early 1950's, while simultaneously becoming a professional jazz pianist, composer and arranger.

In the mid-50's, Mr Schifrin formed his own big concert band in Buenos Aires. After hearing one performance, the legendary trumpeter Dizzy Gillespie asked Mr. Schifrin to become his pianist and arranger. In 1958, Mr Schifrin moved to the United States and thus began a remarkable career.

He has written more than 100 scores and themes for films and television, including "Mission Impossible," "Mannix," "Cool Hand Luke," "Bullitt," and "Dirty Harry."

He served as Musical Director of the Paris Philharmonic Orchestra from 1988 to 1993, recording music for films, performing concerts and participating in television shows.

Since 1989, he has been Music Director of the Glendale Symphony Orchestra, with whom he has premiered several important works.

Among Schifrin's other conducting credits are the London Philharmonic Orchestra, the Los Angeles Philharmonic, the Israel Philharmonic, the Mexico Philharmonic, the London Symphony Orchestra, the Mexico City Philharmonic and the national Symphony Orchestra of Argentina.

Mr. Schifrin is the recipient of many awards and distinctions, including four Grammy Awards and six Oscar nominations. He has been honored by the Israeli Government for his "Contribution to World Understanding Through Music" and appointed "Chevalier de l'Ordre des Arte et Lettres," one of the highest distinctions granted by France's Minister of Culture.

CREATED BY

TIBOR RUDAS

CONCERT GENERAL MANAGER
WAYNE BARUCH

ARTISTS MANAGEMENT
For Mr. Carreras – CARLOS CABALLÉ

For Mr. Domingo – NANCY SELTZER

For Mr. Pavarotti – HERBERT BRESLIN

For Mr. Mehta – GRANT GIFFORD

SPECIAL MEDLEYS & "AVE MARIA" ARRANGED AND ORCHESTRATED BY:
LALO SCHIFRIN

MEMBERS OF THE LOS ANGELES PHILHARMONIC
Managing Director
ERNEST FLEISCHMANN

President of the Board
ROBERT S. ATTIYEH

CHORUS OF THE LOS ANGELES MUSIC CENTER OPERA
General Director
PETER HEMMINGS

Chairman of the Board
BERNARD A. GREENBERG

RECORDINGS
WARNER MUSIC GROUP

COMPACT DISC, CASSETTE, VIDEO AND LASERDISC FORMATS
U.S.A. – ATLANTIC RECORDS AND A* VISION

THE ATLANTIC GROUP

WORLDWIDE – TELDEC CLASSICS INTERNATIONAL

WARNER MUSIC VISION

WORLDWIDE TELEVISION DISTRIBUTION
ALLIED ARTS INTERNATIONAL

VISION HOUSE

RUDAS THEATRICAL ORGANIZATION
President- LEE RUDAS

Executive Vice President- IAN MACLAREN

General Manager- DICK GALLAGHER

Production Supervisor- MATTHIAS SCHREMMER

Office Manager- DAVID ELLIOTT

Assistant to Mr. Rudas- SHELBY GOERLITZ

Assistant to Mr. Rudas- TRACIE CRUZ

Comptroller- DOUG BEISWENGER

Advertising- DEAN RUDAS

Administrative Assistant- DONNA KRASNITZ

Stage Director- THOMAS REITZ

Production Manager- FRANK MILLANE

Lighting Consultant- MONIQUE MILLANE

INTERNATIONAL REPRESENTATIVES
EUROPE- PETER RIEGER KONZERTAGENTUR GMBH

FAR EAST- LUSHINGTON ENTERTAINMENT

UNITED KINGDOM- ALLIED ENTERTAINMENT

HUNGARY- ANDRAS KÜRTHY

JAPAN- HIP PROMOTION

LEGAL COUNSEL
SCHUYLER M. MOORE FOR STROOK, STROOK AND LAVIN

JAY COOPER FOR MANATT, PHELPS & PHILLIPS

NIGEL CLAY FOR GODFREY & ALLEN

EDWIN PERLSTEIN

LOS ANGELES DODGERS, INC.
President- PETER O'MALLEY

Vice President Finance- BOB GRAZIANO

Vice President Ticketing- WALTER NASH

Vice President Stadium Operations- BOB SMITH

Vice President Marketing- BARRY STOCKHAMER

Vice President Communications- TOMMY HAWKINS

Director Ticket Operations- DEBRA DUNCAN

Director M.I.S.- MIKE MULARKY

Assistant Secretary/General Counsel- SANTIAGO FERNANDEZ

STAGE

Art Director- RENÉ LAGLER

Stage Scenery Design- LÁZLÓ SZÉKELY

Lighting Director- OLIN YOUNGER

SOUND

Sound Producer- CHRISTOPHER RAEBURN

Arena Sound Direction- JIMMY LOCK

BY SPECIAL ARRANGEMENT

WITH DECCA RECORDINGS

Sound Engineering Director- JOHN PELLOWE

BY SPECIAL ARRANGEMENT

WITH DECCA RECORDINGS

Sound Design- ALEXANDER YUILL-THORNTON II

Audio Recording Unit- REMOTE RECORDING SERVICES

Post Production- CAPITOL RECORDING STUDIOS, HOLLYWOOD

PRODUCTION SERVICES

Stage- WORLD STAGE, BROWN UNITED

Scaffolding- BROWN UNITED

Sound system provided by- PRO MEDIA, SAN FRANCISCO

Light system provided by- THE ORTE COMPANY, L.A.

Automated Light Systems provided by- VARI LIGHT

Waterfall- SCENIC SERVICES,

PROP SERVICES UNLIMITED

Greens- JACKSON SHRUB SUPPLY

Terrain- FOAM-TEC INC.

Scenic Paintings- JC BACKINGS

Tents- ACADEMY TENT AND CANVAS

Production Consultant- MARK FLAISHER

Event Stage Manager- JOSEPH PARDIEU

Host Management- RON AND ORLLYENE WALKER

Security- SPECIAL SECURITY SERVICES, GERMANY

MARTIN HOUBE, JENS KRÜGER

Insurance- ROBERTSON & TAYLOR

Public Relations- T. PATRICK, INC.,

LAISTER-DICKSON

Merchandising-

WINTERLAND

(NORTH & SOUTH AMERICA & FAR EAST)

EVENT! (U.K. & EUROPE)

PLAYBILL (AUSTRALASIA)

Charity Dinner- LEVY/PAZANTI

TELEVISION

Director- BILL COSEL

Coordinating Producer- GEOFF BENNETT

Technical Director- JOHN FIELD

Television Production Consultants- ROCKY OLDHAM, MALCOM GERRIE

Executive Producer- Warner Music Vision - RAY STILL

TV Audio- ED GREENE

Associate Director- CHRISTINE CLARK

Video Facilities- G.C. & COMPANY

Post Production- COMPLETE POST, INC., L.A.

DOCUMENTARY

Created and Produced by- TIBOR RUDAS

Concept and Script by- WAYNE BARUCH

Narrated by- ROGER MOORE

Executive Producer- DAVID DINKINS JR.

WORLD CUP USA 1994

Chairman & CEO- ALAN ROTHENBERG

Managing Director & COO- SCOTT PARKS LETELLIER

Managing Director & CAO- ELI PRIMROSE-SMITH

Executive Vice President- DOUG ARNOT

Executive Vice President- SUNIL GULATI

Executive Vice President- MARLA MESSING

Sr. Vice President/General Counsel- LEAH TUFFANELLI

Vice President Business Affairs- TONY TOLBERT

Assistant V.P. Client Services- SHANNON VUKALCIC

Manager Special Events Ticketing- TOM PACE

Special Thanks to- FÉDÉRATION INTERNATIONALE

DE FOOTBALL ASSOCIATION

SPECIAL THANKS

To our friends at Warner Music Group:

ROBERT J. MORGADO, AHMET ERTEGUN,

DOUG MORRIS, RAMON LOPEZ, PETER ANDRY,

VAL AZZOLI, TRACY NICHOLAS BLEDSOE,

JAMES CARRADINE, KAREN COLAMUSSI,

PATTE CONTE, VICKY GERMAISE,

STUART HIRSCH, PETER IKIN, MELVYN LEWINTER,

ANNE-MARIE NICOL, JORDAN ROST, SANDY SAWOTKA,

RAY STILL, and MARGARET WADE.

PUBLISHED BY
Collins Publishers San Francisco

DESIGN
Pentagram Design, Austin

TEXT BY
Sam Paul and Wayne Baruch

RESEARCH
Philip Caggiano

TEXT TRANSLATIONS
Direct Language Communications, Inc.
Dale MacAdoo
Gery Bramall

PRINTED IN THE USA BY
Hennegan, Cincinnati, Ohio

PHOTOGRAPHY & ILLUSTRATION CREDITS

MAJOR PHOTOGRAPHY
Richard Haughton, Pages: 1, 2/3, 6/7, 15, 22, 34, 35, 36/37, 38/39, 42, 43, 46, 47, 52, 53, 54/55, 56/57, 60, 61, 66, 67, 68, 69, 72, 73, 74/75, 76/77, 116, 118, 119

David Kennerly, Pages: 8, 14, 16/17, 32/33, 35, 40, 42, 43, 50/51, 61, 62/63, 64/65, 70/71, 78/79, 80/81, 117, 126/127

Gerd Ludwig, Pages: 4/5, 10, 42, 44/45, 48/49, 52, 58/59, 82/83, 120/121, 126, 127

PAGE 11
Vince Compagnone, courtesy of the L.A. Times

PAGE 12-13
Henry Grossman

PAGE 18
Robert Cahen

PAGE 19
Top right: Robert Cahen
Middle left: Winnie Klotz/Metropolitan Opera
Bottom right: © Steve J. Sherman

PAGE 22
Middle left: Robert Cahen
Below: Robert Cahen

PAGE 23
Top left: Robert Cahen
Middle right: Marty Sohl

PAGE 24-25
Vittoriano Rastelli

PAGE 26
Top right: Robert Cahen
Middle left: Robert Cahen

PAGE 27
Middle right: Robert Cahen
Bottom: © Steve J. Sherman

PAGE 26-27
Masami Hotta

PAGE 28-29
© Steve J. Sherman

PAGE 30
Top right: © Jack Vartoogian
Middle left: Courtesy of Zubin Mehta

PAGE 31
Top: Courtesy of Zubin Mehta
Bottom: © Steve J. Sherman

PAGE 43
Top right: Robert Cahen

PAGES 84 THROUGH 115:
Illustrations by Anthony Russo

LIBRETTO CREDITS

PAGE 88
O Souverain! O Juge! O Pere!
Furnished by Sony Classical
English translation: Thomas G. Kaufman
German translation: Ingrid Trautmann

PAGE 90
Quando Le Sere Al Placido
Original text reprinted by kind permission of Sony Classical GmbH
English translation by kind permission of Gwyn Morris

PAGE 92
Porquoi Me Reveller
English translation by kind permission of The Decca Record Company Ltd.
The original text is out of copyright.

PAGE 94
With a Song in My Heart
© 1929 (Renewed) Warner Bros. Inc. & Williamson Music Company
All Rights Reserved. Used by permission.

PAGE 96
Granada (Fantasía Española)
© 1932 Peer International Corporation (Copyright Renewed)
© 1950 Southern Music Publishing Co. (A/Asia) Pty. Ltd.
International Copyright Secured
Made in USA. All Rights Reserved.
Used by permission of CPP/Belwin, Inc., Miami, FL 33014
Music and Spanish lyric: Agustín Lara
English translation: Dorothy Dodd

PAGE 98
Non Ti Scordar Di Me
© 1935 (Renewed) Beboton Verlag GMBH
All rights on behalf of Beboton Verlag GMBH administered by Chappell & Co.
All Rights Reserved. Used by permission.
English translation: Avril Bardoni
German translation: Gery Bramall
French translation: Rosine Fitzgerald

PAGE 100
Tu, Ca Nun Chiagne
English translation: Avril Bardoni

PAGE 102
Amor, Vida De Mi Vida
Furnished by EMI Classics
English translation: Lionel Salter
French translation: Michael Roubinet

PAGE 104
Ave Maria
Permission granted by Decca Record Company for translations.

PAGE 106
E Lucevan Le Stelle
Italian translation: Libretto: Illica & Giacosa
English translation furnished by EMI Classics

PAGE 108
Vesti La Giubba
Texts and English, French and German translations reprinted by kind permission of Deutsche Grammophon GMBH, Hamburg
English translation: Lionel Salter
German translation: Ludwig Hartmann
French translation: Antoine Vierne

PAGE 110
Nessun Dorma!
Permission granted by Decca Record Company Limited for original and English translation.
English translation: Laura Mardon

PAGE 112
La Donna É Mobile
Translation by Dale MacAdoo
Reprinted by courtesy of EMI Classics

PAGE 114
Libiamo, Ne' Lieti Calici ("Brindisi")
Translation by Gery Bramall
Reprinted by kind permission of Teldec Classics International

First published in the USA in 1994 by

Collins Publishers San Francisco

1160 Battery Street, San Francisco, CA 94111

©1994 Collins Publishers San Francisco

Text: Sam Paul with Wayne Baruch

Book and Jacket Design: Pentagram Design, Austin

Major Photography: Richard Haughton,

David Kennerly and

Gerd Ludwig

Library of Congress Cataloging-in-Publication Data

3 Tenors in Concert 1994

Program of a concert held in Dodger Stadium, Los Angeles, Calif.

on July 16, 1994.

At head of title:

Tibor Rudas presents Carreras, Domingo, Pavarotti, with Mehta.

ISBN 0-00-225030-6

1. Concert programs – California – Los Angeles.

2. Carreras, José – Performances – California – Los Angeles.

3. Domingo, Plácido – Performances – California – Los Angeles.

4. Pavarotti, Luciano – Performances – California – Los Angeles.

I. Rudas, Tibor.

II. Title Tibor Rudas presents Carreras, Domingo, Pavarotti, Mehta.

ML42.L78D5 1994

782.1'078'79494–dc20

94-24790

CIP

MN

Printed in U. S. A. by Hennegan

1 3 5 7 9 8 6 4 2